ZERO TRUST PRIVACY
A new strategy for protecting y

Nandor Feher

Published on 09/28/2023.

First Edition

About the Author: Nandor Feher

Nandor Feher is a professional with more than 17 years of experience in Information Security. He currently holds the position of CISO and DPO at Positivo Tecnologia, one of the largest hardware manufacturers in the world.

Nandor holds a degree in Computer Networks and Information Security from Uniasselvi and holds more than thirteen certifications in privacy, risk, management, and governance, including CISSP, CISM, CISO, CRISC, CDPSE, DPO, ISO 27001, PDPP, PDPF, Security+, Cloud+, CSCP, among others.

Throughout his career, Nandor has been head of Information Security at renowned multinationals such as Tigre Tubos e Conexões, and Grupo Lunelli. In his career, he has walked a comprehensive journey in technology, ranging from microcomputer support to infrastructure. This vast understanding of the different technological aspects and his long journey in cybersecurity, led him to realize that digital security is more than a mere technical requirement, but a critical business strategy.

Deeply influenced by his mother, who always taught him the art of questioning, Nandor faced significant challenges, such as modernizing technologies in established companies. With dexterity, patience, and strategic vision, he overcame resistance while remaining focused on making cybersecurity a strategic cornerstone.

His vast expertise extends from leadership, governance, operations, risk management to privacy. With important deliveries in the sector, he led a cybersecurity maturity journey, elevating the information security program from basic controls to management with strategic alignment based on risk. In addition, Nandor successfully led the company in adapting to the requirements of the LGPD.

Moreover, to his professional responsibilities, Nandor is an ardent advocate for information security. Its mission is clear: to make people's lives better through technology, but always safely. He believes that, through training and awareness, one can promote a use of technologies that is both balanced and safe.

At every stage of his life, professional or personal, Nandor relentlessly pursues excellence, growth, and deep understanding.

International recognition

In 2023, Nandor Feher was recognized as one of the top 100 CISOs in the world. This is an important recognition of Nandor's work and dedication to information security.

Contribution to the Cybersecurity Community

In addition to actively participating in the development of exams for ISC2, receiving the title of "Cybersecurity Exam Development Volunteer", Nandor also conducts training and lectures. In doing so, he shares and disseminates the knowledge he has gained over the years, further strengthening the cybersecurity community.

1. Introduction

In an interconnected world, the line between digital and physical space has become increasingly blurred. Every action we take online, whether it is a post on a social network, a purchase in an online store, or a simple search, generates a digital footprint. This data, when collected and analyzed, can reveal a lot about an individual, from their spending habits to their political opinions.

However, with the increase in data collection, so too does the concern about privacy. Regardless of their size, businesses are now subject to cyberattacks, which often lead to sensitive data being compromised.

How do you ensure that personal data does not fall into the wrong hands? How do you ensure that the information you collect is used ethically and responsibly? This is where the concept of Zero Trust Privacy comes in. This approach, which is based on the principle of "never trust, always verify," promises to be the answer to many of the privacy challenges we face today.

In this eBook, we will explore what Zero Trust Privacy is, why it is crucial in today's digital age, and how organizations can implement it to protect their users' data. If you are an information security professional, privacy professional, or simply an enthusiast who wants to better understand how your data is protected, this guide is for you.

As we move forward in exploring the mysteries of Zero Trust Privacy, we will take a unique approach to make it easier for you to understand. Imagine that we are building a castle, a fortress of protection. This metaphor of the castle will serve as a guide, illuminating the concepts and practices of this universe. It will help us visualize challenges and solutions in a vivid and tangible way. Thus, as you proceed with this reading, you will not only be absorbing information but also being transported to an engaging narrative that will enrich your learning experience. Get ready for a journey that goes beyond the conventional.

2. History and Evolution of Data Privacy

Privacy, as a concept, has deep roots in human history. Since the earliest days of civilizations, people have valued their privacy, whether in personal conversations, handwritten letters, or secret diaries. However, the digital revolution has radically transformed our perception and management of privacy.

During my high school years, I remember that girls' diaries were considered treasure troves of information. These handwritten records contained everything from culinary preferences, accounts of youthful passions to aspirations for the future, and opinions about classmates and teachers. Only extremely trustworthy individuals had the privilege of accessing these secrets, were carefully guarded and, when shared, came with an oath of discretion. At that time, without realizing it, I was already being introduced to the concepts of information security and privacy.

In the United States, the 1970s were a pivotal period for data privacy. With increasing digitization, it became apparent that personal data was at risk. The creation of the *Fair Information Practice Principles* (FIPPs) by the *U.S. Department of Health, Education, and Welfare* was one of the first efforts to address these concerns. These initial guidelines emphasized transparency, data integrity, and the right of individuals to access and correct their information.

Europe, recognizing the importance of privacy in the digital age, has taken significant steps to protect the rights of its citizens. The General Data Protection Regulation (GDPR) of 2018 was a milestone. Not only has it established clear rights for European citizens, but it has also influenced privacy legislation around the world.

Inspired by the GDPR, Brazil's General Data Protection Law (LGPD) was signed into law in 2018. This legislation reflects a global trend of strengthening citizens' privacy and establishes clear guidelines for the collection, storage, and processing of personal data in Brazil.

2.1. The Rise of Zero Trust

With the increasing complexity of the digital landscape and ever-evolving threats, the need for a more robust approach to privacy has arisen. The Zero Trust model, which originated in the field of cybersecurity, has begun to be seen as a promising solution to modern privacy challenges.

The Zero Trust approach represents a paradigmatic shift in how organizations perceive and approach security and privacy. Its emergence and popularization are not coincidences, but rather a direct response to the evolution of the digital landscape.

Origins in Cybersecurity: The concept of Zero Trust was initially introduced in the context of cybersecurity. The core idea was that organizations should not automatically trust anything, internally or externally, but rather verify everything before granting access. This approach was a direct response to the recognition that threats could come from both outside and inside an organization.

Adapting to Data Privacy: The rise in data breaches and growing data privacy awareness have prompted the adaptation of Zero Trust to address specific privacy challenges. Rather than focusing solely on security threats, Zero Trust Privacy focuses on ensuring that data is accessed and utilized responsibly and securely, regardless of where it is stored or who is trying to access it.

In recent years, several factors have contributed to the rise of Zero Trust as a trend in the approach to privacy, some of them are:

Increased Insider Threats: Recognizing that not all threats come from the outside, organizations have begun to adopt Zero Trust to mitigate risks associated with malicious or negligent employees.

IT Infrastructure Complexity: With the adoption of multiple cloud solutions, *IoT* devices, and decentralized networks, organizations have faced the challenge of securing increasingly complex environments. Zero Trust Privacy offers a unified approach that can be applied across distinct parts of an infrastructure.

Privacy Regulations: As mentioned earlier, regulations such as GDPR and LGPD emphasize the need to protect citizens' data. Zero Trust, with its rigorous approach, helps organizations meet these regulatory requirements.

Adopting Zero Trust Privacy is not just about improving data security. There are several other benefits that organizations can take advantage of.

Identifying Privacy Risks: Zero Trust Privacy can identify privacy risks throughout the organization, ensuring that no area is overlooked.

Increased Customer Trust and Revenue: By reducing privacy risks, organizations can increase customer trust, which in turn can lead to an increase in revenue.

Financial Posture Support: Zero Trust Privacy strengthens the organization's financial posture by preventing unexpected costs associated with data breaches.

Data as a Foundation: Using data as a foundation minimizes rework and infrastructure changes that often lead to unplanned costs and time investment.

Strengthening Personal Data Protection: Zero Trust Privacy also strengthens the security protections of all personal data, thereby limiting the potential for breaches or fines.

3. The Concept of Zero Trust Privacy

As we have seen before, we are living in a time when threats to privacy are constantly evolving, the traditional approach to data protection often proves to be insufficient. Zero Trust Privacy has emerged as a solution, proposing a profound change in how we view and manage data privacy.

3.1. The Analogy of the Ancient Vase

To better understand what Zero Trust Privacy is, imagine an antique and precious vase in a museum. Traditionally, this vase would be protected by a single barrier: a glass display case. However, if someone managed to break this display case, the vase would be vulnerable. Zero Trust Privacy proposes a different approach. Instead of a single barrier, we would have multiple sensors, alarms, and surveillance systems, all working together to protect the vessel. Every move would be monitored, and nothing would be assumed to be safe by default.

One of the most relevant approaches is context- and temporality-based access. This means that in addition to determining who can have access to an object, such as a vase, it also considers when and under what conditions that access is allowed. In more sophisticated models, one can even define which specific parts of the vase someone is allowed to touch. In the traditional system of protection, anyone who was inside the museum and possessed the key to the display case would have unrestricted access to the vase, regardless of the time or circumstance.

The essence of Zero Trust Privacy is simple: trust nothing by default. Every data access, every transaction, and every interaction must be verified and authenticated. This means that even internal users and systems are not automatically trusted. They must prove their identity and intentions at every turn.

3.2. The Evolution of Zero Trust

The concept of Zero Trust is not new. It originated in the field of cybersecurity, focusing on protecting against internal and external threats. However, with the rise in privacy concerns, Zero Trust has evolved to address not only security but also data privacy.

While Zero Trust is poised to become the standard approach to cybersecurity, many security professionals see it as just a "marketing gimmick." However, the modern definition of Zero Trust is clear:

"Zero Trust is a cybersecurity concept centered on the principle that organizations should not, by default, trust anything inside or outside their perimeters, and instead should check anything and everything that attempts to connect to their systems before granting access."

In other words, Zero Trust Privacy is a privacy model that denies access to data by default. Prevention of threats or misuse is achieved by granting access utilizing policies informed by continuous, contextual, and risk-based scanning for users and their associated devices.

The core principles of Zero Trust are:
- Deny by default.
- Access by policy only.
- Applicable to data, workloads, users, and devices.
- Least privilege access.
- Security monitoring.
- Risk-based verification.

While Zero Trust fundamentally changes security protocols, it is important to note that Zero Trust is not a security awareness and training strategy. There is no need for most of an organization's end users to be familiar with this concept. In fact, pushing Zero Trust concepts onto end users can be counterproductive, as the perception of having "zero trust" implies a lack of trust in employees.

But is it worth using a zero-trust privacy concept in my company?

To answer this question, it is important to understand the fundamental concepts and advantages of this approach.

Zero Trust Privacy is an approach that redefines the way organizations perceive and approach data security and privacy. Let us explore its fundamental concepts and the benefits they bring to organizations.

Fundamental Concepts of Zero Trust Privacy:

Data-Centric Approach: Zero Trust Privacy highlights the importance of data as the building block of security. Recognizes that organizations must protect and monitor data and related activities to effectively meet stringent privacy requirements.

Micro Perimeter Approach: Unlike traditional perimeter-based security, Zero Trust Privacy promotes a 'micro-perimeter' approach. This means that access to the data is only for what is strictly necessary, based on factors such as the purpose of the processing, user access permissions, data location, and policies.

Continuous Authentication: Zero Trust Privacy incorporates continuous authentication to verify the identity and trustworthiness of users throughout their session. This helps prevent unauthorized access and reduces the risk of data breaches.

Access Controls: Zero Trust Privacy involves implementing granular access controls to ensure that users only have access to the resources they need. This approach minimizes the potential impact of a security breach and reduces the attack surface.

Privacy Management: Zero Trust Privacy solutions often include privacy management capabilities that allow organizations to apply granular controls to data and ensure compliance with privacy policies and regulations for the data subject.

Benefits of Zero Trust Privacy:

Advanced Data Protection: By focusing on data-centric security, Zero Trust Privacy offers enhanced protection for sensitive data.

Reduced Risk of Data Breaches: Continuous authentication and granular access controls help reduce the risk of unauthorized access and data breaches.

Compliance with Privacy Regulations: Zero Trust Privacy solutions often include privacy management features that help organizations comply with privacy regulations such as GDPR, POPIA, PDPA, HIPAA, CPRA, PIPA, and others.

Enhanced Visibility and Control: Zero Trust Privacy gives organizations better visibility into data and related activities, allowing for enhanced control over privacy and security.

4. Why Zero Trust Privacy Is Indispensable Now

Technology advances by leaps and bounds, bringing innovations and opportunities. However, with these advances also come new threats and challenges. Data privacy has become a minefield, with data breaches and privacy abuses are now commonplace.

4.1 Driving Competitive Differentials:

How can an effective privacy program based on Zero Trust Privacy elevate your business?

Privacy is not just a matter of compliance or data protection; It can serve as a significant competitive differentiator for organizations. When implemented effectively, privacy operations can bring both tangible and intangible benefits to the business. Here are seven business benefits that result from effective privacy operations:

1. Meeting Customer Compliance and Contractual Privacy Requirements: Ensuring that the organization is complying with local and

international regulations and meeting the contractual requirements set forth by customers.

2. Data Breach Prevention: Protect the organization and its individuals from potential harm resulting from data breaches by ensuring the integrity and confidentiality of information.

3. Maintaining and Improving Brand Value and Customer Loyalty: Effective privacy management can improve brand perception and strengthen customer loyalty.

4. Strengthening and Growing Business Innovation: With privacy guaranteed, businesses can innovate with confidence, knowing that customer data is protected.

5. Maintaining Public, Investor, and Customer Trust: Trust is an intangible but crucial asset, and effective privacy management can strengthen that trust.

6. Gaining a Competitive Advantage: In a saturated market, privacy can be the differentiator that puts an organization ahead of its competitors.

7. Reduced Business Transactional Costs: Effective privacy operations can lead to more efficient processes and, consequently, lower transactional costs.

Value is built on top of existing business management and production best practices. When privacy differentiators help an organization gain a competitive advantage, they elevate the organization to a new level of excellence and recognition in the marketplace.

4.2. The Age of Artificial Intelligence

Artificial Intelligence (AI) carries the potential to redefine diverse industries, from medicine to transportation, bringing unprecedented optimizations and innovations. But like every revolution, it comes with its concerns and challenges, especially related to data privacy and security.

AI's ability to probe and decipher vast datasets can lead to valuable discoveries, but also privacy breaches.

Facial recognition, for example, is widely disseminated using AI, and this technology, while useful, can be exploited to track individuals without their permission. In addition, this data is commonly classified as critical in major privacy legislations around the world.

With AI, it is possible to create detailed profiles of users based on their online behavior, which can result in excessive advertising or even discrimination.

As AI becomes increasingly accessible, information security becomes a concern. It is common for sensitive data such as passwords or access keys to be inadvertently shared during interactions with AI systems. A single security lapse or system vulnerability can compromise the entire structure of an organization.

With the accelerated movement to create platforms using AI, many of these tools do not offer robust privacy guarantees, leaving personal and corporate data exposed. The growing wave of AI-related apps and extensions can be a gateway to security vulnerabilities, especially if they come from dubious sources.

It is also common for these platforms to be published without proper security testing. If you are curious to know more about the subject, on my LinkedIn profile I have articles talking a little more about this movement.

AI as a powerful and ever-evolving tool can also be used to carry out phishing attacks and social engineering techniques, becoming more cunning. This requires users to be constantly vigilant so as not to be scammed.

The storage of information generated by Artificial Intelligence (AI) poses a significant challenge in terms of security. Given the sensitive and often critical nature of data processed and produced by AI systems, any failure in the storage protocol can result in unwanted exposures. Without robust protection measures and secure protocols, crucial data is at risk of being compromised, leading to potentially devastating consequences for the organizations and individuals involved.

Not only do insecure devices and networks pose risks in themselves, but in environments influenced by Artificial

Intelligence (AI), these vulnerabilities can have amplified consequences. AI, with its ability to process and analyze large volumes of data quickly, can be exploited by malicious actors if it is not adequately protected. In addition, the use of inappropriate or easily crackable passwords on platforms that employ AI further broadens the spectrum of threats. These platforms, which often have access to sensitive information and make decisions based on complex algorithms, when compromised, can cause significant harm. Therefore, it is especially important for companies to adopt robust cybersecurity practices, especially in environments where AI plays a central role.

4.3. The Digitalization of Enterprises

As more companies embark on the digital transformation journey, the amount of data they collect, and store explodes. Many of these companies still rely on traditional approaches to privacy, which may prove insufficient in today's landscape. The Zero Trust Privacy approach can offer a robust solution to these challenges.

Digital transformation is a double-edged sword, having many benefits but adding new risks. While businesses benefit from the efficiency and insights afforded by digitization, they also become more attractive targets for cybercriminals due to the vast amount of data they have online.

There are major security challenges where many companies are moving to the cloud and adopting IoT solutions, increasing the attack surface and making traditional security strategies obsolete.

4.4. Data Breaches: A Growing Threat

Almost every day, we hear news of new data breaches, where personal information of thousands or even millions of people is exposed. These breaches not only damage the reputation of the companies involved, but also jeopardize consumer trust in the digital world.

The frequency and scale of data breaches in modern times are, in fact, alarming, and the financial impact of these breaches goes far beyond the direct costs associated with managing and recovering from a breach. In addition to immediate revenue losses, businesses also face long-term consequences. Customer trust, once shaken, can take years to restore, impacting loyalty and retention. Outages resulting from breaches can cause significant delays in strategic projects, in some cases forcing the cancellation of planned improvements in various areas of the organization. Human resources are also affected, with internal teams being diverted from their regular roles to deal with the crisis, driving up operating costs. Companies often need to hire specialized consultancies to respond to and mitigate the damage, an additional expense that, given the urgency, can be high. In the financial scenario, the company's reputation may suffer, leading to a devaluation of its shares on the stock exchange. In summary, the ramifications of a data breach are vast, permeating nearly every aspect of an organization.

We know that trust is an intangible but vital asset for any organization. Once lost, it can be extremely difficult to win back. Customers and partners who realize that their sensitive information is not being handled with proper care can quickly take their business elsewhere. Additionally, privacy regulations are becoming increasingly stringent in many jurisdictions, and failure to comply can result in substantial fines.

In an environment where AI and technology play increasingly central roles, the need for robust security and privacy measures is more critical than ever. It is not just about protecting data and systems, it is about preserving brand reputation, customer loyalty, and ultimately, the long-term viability of the organization. Taking a proactive, principled approach like Zero Trust Privacy can be a vital step in building a security posture that protects not only the tangible assets but also the trust and reputation that are critical to continued success.

4.5. The Need for a New Approach

With the constant evolution of cyber threats and the increasing complexity of networks and systems, it is clear that traditional approaches to privacy and security no longer seem to be enough. Zero Trust Privacy emerges not only as an option, but as a methodology that can help any organization that wishes to protect its users' data in today's digital world.

The current scenario requires a deep re-evaluation of privacy and security strategies, as we may have serious limitations in traditional approaches.

Permission-based systems and firewalls, which were once the backbone of cybersecurity, are no longer enough. Attackers are using more sophisticated tactics, exploiting vulnerabilities, and finding ways to bypass these defenses. Traditional approaches often fail to detect and prevent breaches, leaving organizations exposed to significant risks.

By adopting the principle of "never trust, always verify," Zero Trust Privacy offers a proactive and dynamic approach. This means that each access request is authenticated, continuously validated, and evaluated based on a variety of factors. This granular approach ensures that access is granted only when it is properly justified, minimizing the attack surface.

Zero Trust Privacy is not a one-size-fits-all solution; It is an ongoing process that requires constant monitoring, evaluation, and adaptation. As new threats emerge and technologies evolve, Zero Trust policies and controls must be adjusted to ensure they remain effective.

5. Implementing Zero Trust Privacy

The adoption of Zero Trust Privacy is a strategic approach that seeks a fundamental shift in the way organizations manage data privacy and security. The transition to Zero Trust Privacy is not just about integrating new tools or technologies; It is a journey that requires meticulous planning, execution, and continuous evaluation.

As you embark on the journey to implement Zero Trust Privacy, be prepared to face major challenges.

Cultural Resistance:

People are naturally resistant to change, and this is especially true for changes that may seem restrictive or intrusive. It is important to explain to employees, leaders, and stakeholders why Zero Trust Privacy is necessary and how it will help them stay secure.

The key is education and awareness. Workshops, trainings, and internal campaigns can help highlight the importance of Zero Trust and the need for change.

Beyond simply explaining, it is important to involve employees and leaders in the implementation process. This will help them feel more engaged in the process and more likely to support it.

It is important to be patient and persistent when implementing Zero Trust Privacy. It may take time for employees and leaders to adapt to the new approach.

Technical Complexity:

Starting small by focusing on critical areas first and then gradually expanding the implementation can prove to be a highly effective strategy. Also, consider seeking external advice or ready-made solutions that ease the transition.

Implementing Zero Trust Privacy can be a technical challenge, especially for organizations with legacy infrastructures or interconnected systems. It is important to have a comprehensive plan for implementation and ensure that you have the necessary resources and expertise to execute it.

It is important to be flexible and be prepared to make adjustments to the plan as needed. The security landscape is constantly changing, and it is important to ensure that your Zero Trust Privacy approach is adapting as well.

Associated Costs:

Implementing Zero Trust Privacy can require significant investments in new technologies, training, and resources. Conducting a cost-benefit analysis is crucial to ensure the benefits outweigh the costs.

In addition to cost-benefit analysis, an important strategy is to consider the potential cost of data breaches or regulatory non-compliance. In many cases, the initial investment can result in significant savings in the long term.

Maintain Usability:

With constant checks and strict authentication, there can be a concern that the user experience will suffer. It is important to implement user-friendly authentication solutions that balance security and usability.

For example, you can use context-based multi-factor authentication, which requires users to provide more than one form of authentication, depending on the context of the request. This can help improve security without significantly hindering the user experience.

Imagine you are about to embark on an expedition to build a fortified City in an unfamiliar land. This City is not like any other City; It is designed to be extremely secure in a world full of uncertainty and threats. The construction of this City is like the implementation of Zero Trust Privacy.

Embarking on the Zero Trust Privacy journey is like starting the construction of this fortified City. It is not just about erecting high walls and sturdy gates; It is about understanding the terrain, getting to know the inhabitants, and being prepared to adapt to change.

Just as every stone placed on the city wall is meticulously chosen and positioned, every step in adopting Zero Trust Privacy requires planning and consideration. Cultural resistance within an organization can be likened to the initial inhabitants of the earth, who may be skeptical or resistant to the idea of changing their traditional way of living. Through education, training, and involvement, we can gain their support, just as a wise leader would gain the trust of his people.

Technical complexity is like the challenging terrain that the city must be built on. There may be steep mountains, rushing rivers, or dense forests. However, with the right strategy, proper tools, and expertise, we can turn these challenges into defensive advantages for our city.

The costs associated with building the city are similar to the investments required to implement Zero Trust Privacy. While there may be a significant upfront cost, the long-term benefits – a thriving and secure City or a protected digital environment – are worth the investment.

And, of course, we cannot forget the City's inhabitants. Just as usability is crucial to Zero Trust Privacy, life inside the fortified City must be enjoyable and functional for its inhabitants. There is no point in having impenetrable walls if the people inside them are not happy or cannot live productively.

Over the next few chapters, we will continue to explore this metaphor of the fortified City, guiding you through the ins and outs of implementing Zero Trust Privacy, from initial planning to ongoing maintenance and evaluation. Just as building a city is an ongoing journey, implementing Zero Trust Privacy is an evolving process that requires ongoing vigilance, adaptation, and commitment.

5.1. Definition of a Strategy

Implementing Zero Trust Privacy starts with defining a clear strategy. This strategy should articulate the organization's objectives regarding Zero Trust Privacy, outline the risks it aims to mitigate, and specify the resources necessary for its implementation. The strategy serves as a roadmap for the journey, guiding the organization through each step of the process.

It is important to stay focused, and you should develop a security strategy that focuses on protecting data and ensuring privacy. This strategy should be aligned with the organization's business objectives, considering industry-specific threats and vulnerabilities.

Think of the fortified City as an emerging kingdom that wants to establish itself as a dominant power in the region. To do this, the kingdom needs a strategic plan.

Defining a Strategy: This is the king's vision and his advice for the future of the kingdom. They gather in the great hall, unroll a map of the region, and begin to lay out their plan. Where will they build outposts? What trade routes will they establish? What alliances will they form? This is their roadmap to success.

Clear Objectives: Just as the king wants to expand his territory, secure lucrative trade routes, and form beneficial alliances, the organization needs to have clear objectives for Zero Trust Privacy. It could be protecting certain critical data, ensuring compliance with specific regulations, or improving customer trust.

Resources Needed: In the same way that the kingdom needs masons to build its walls, soldiers to defend its borders, and diplomats to negotiate alliances, the organization needs to identify the resources – be they technological, human, or financial – that will be needed to implement its Zero Trust Privacy strategy.

Specific Threats and Vulnerabilities: Just as the realm needs to be aware of neighboring kingdoms that may be hostile or trade routes that may be ambushed by bad guys, the organization needs to understand the threats specific to its industry and how Zero Trust Privacy can help mitigate those risks.

In this metaphor, strategy is the kingdom's comprehensive plan to ensure its success and safety. Without a clear strategy, the kingdom may find itself unprepared for the challenges it faces, whether it is an invasion of a neighboring kingdom or an internal uprising. Similarly, without a well-defined Zero Trust Privacy strategy, the organization may find itself vulnerable to threats and challenges in the digital world.

5.2. Identification of Compliance Requirements

Before taking any steps forward, it is important for the organization to deeply recognize and understand its compliance requirements. These requirements are shaped by laws, regulations, and standards that provide clear guidelines for managing and protecting personal and sensitive data.

Finally, it is essential to reflect on the company's internal policies. The organization must evaluate how its operations and business model align with or are impacted by specific regulations. This analysis will ensure that the company not only complies with external regulations but is also in tune with its own internal principles and guidelines.

Imagine the fortified city again, but this time, think of it as a kingdom that borders several other kingdoms. Each of these neighboring kingdoms has its own sets of laws and business agreements that affect the way the city interacts with them.

Compliance Requirements: These are like the treaties and agreements that the city has with its neighbors. Before a city can trade or interact with a neighboring kingdom, it needs to understand and respect the laws and customs of that kingdom. If a neighboring kingdom has strict rules about importing certain goods, the city needs to be aware of this and act accordingly.

Internal Policies: In the same way that the city has its own internal laws and regulations—such as rules about commerce, fees, and security—the organization has its internal policies. These are the rules that govern the day-to-day life of the city, regardless of treaties with neighboring kingdoms. For example, even if a neighboring kingdom allows the sale of a certain product, the city may have its own rules prohibiting it.

Alignment with Regulations: Just as a wise king would consult with his advisors before making a deal with a neighboring kingdom, to ensure that it does not conflict with the city's internal laws, the organization needs to ensure that its efforts to comply with external regulations do not conflict with its internal policies.

In this metaphor, the city, by understanding and respecting both external treaties and its own internal laws, ensures that its interactions with neighboring kingdoms are harmonious and beneficial, while maintaining order and security within its own walls. Similarly, an organization that understands its compliance requirements and internal policies is better positioned to operate effectively and ethically on the global stage.

5.3. Data Inventory and Mapping

With the strategy formed and compliance requirements in mind, the organization must then undertake its efforts on a comprehensive inventory of data. This involves identifying all the personal and sensitive data being processed, determining its location, access permissions, usage, and purpose.

Organizations need to identify and classify their data to understand what and how needs to be protected. This involves deep work where a complete mapping of the data flow is expected as a result, identifying where the data is stored, who has access to it and how it is used.

Imagine the fortified city as a sprawling metropolis, with diverse districts, markets, homes, and hidden treasures. Before he can effectively protect the city, the ruler needs to know exactly what is inside its walls.

Data Inventory: This is the equivalent of conducting a complete census of the city. Every citizen, every merchant, every precious stone hidden in the coffers is accounted for. The king sends his scribes and accountants to every corner of the city to make a detailed record of all that is valuable.

Data Location: Just as the king needs to know where every treasure is hidden, organizations need to know where their data is stored. In our city, this may involve mapping out every house, every market, every hiding place.

Access to Data: In the same way that the monarch needs to know who has the key to each vault or treasure, organizations need to identify who has access to each set of data. In the city, this may involve checking which merchants are allowed to sell in which markets or which guards have the key to which gates.

Use of Data: Just as the king wants to know what each building is used for (whether it is a house, a warehouse, or a market), organizations need to understand how data is used. In our metaphor, this might involve understanding which markets sell which goods or which artisans produce which products.

By the end of this meticulous census, the city ruler will have a clear view of all its assets and resources. He will know where the vulnerable points are, where the treasures are hidden, and who has access to them. Similarly, after data inventory and mapping, organizations will have a clear understanding of their data, allowing them to protect it more effectively.

5.4. Designation of a Protective Surface

Once the data has been mapped and understood in its entirety, the next crucial step is the designation of a "protective surface." This concept refers to the identification and delineation of the most critical and sensitive systems, applications, and resources within the organization.

The protective surface is not just limited to digital systems or databases. It can also encompass communications, network infrastructures, access points, and any other resource that is critical to the organization's operations.

Under the Zero Trust Privacy paradigm, it is vital that this protection surface is rigorously defended, monitored, and updated. This means that any access to it, whether internal or external, must be meticulously authenticated, validated, and monitored. The idea is to minimize the attack surface by limiting opportunities for malicious actors to exploit vulnerabilities.

By properly designating and protecting this surface, the organization establishes a robust line of defense, ensuring that the most valuable and sensitive assets are safeguarded under the most stringent privacy and security guidelines.

Think of the "protective surface" as the heart of an ancient fortified city. Within the city walls, there are several buildings, streets, and squares, but the castle in the center is the most protected and valuable. This castle, with its watchtowers, moats, and reinforced gates, represents the organization's protective surface. Just as the castle guards would meticulously check each visitor, allowing entry only to those who have permission, the protective surface ensures that only trusted entities have access to the most critical assets. And just as the castle walls are constantly monitored and reinforced to resist new threats, the protective surface must also be continually upgraded and defended. In a world filled with ever-evolving challenges and threats, it is essential that the heart of the organization – its protective surface – remains unshaken and impenetrable.

5.5. Implementation of Identity and Access Controls

Once the protection surface is established, the next critical step is the implementation of robust identity and access controls. These controls are the front line in defending against threats, ensuring that only authorized individuals can access critical information and systems.

Multi-factor authentication (MFA) is one of the most effective tools in this context. By requiring multiple forms of verification — such as something the user knows (password), something they own (a token or smartphone), and something they are (fingerprint or facial recognition) — MFA makes it harder for attackers to gain access, even if they have stolen credentials.

In addition to MFA, it is essential to establish access policies based on roles or responsibilities. This means that users only have access to the systems and information that are strictly necessary for their roles. For example, an employee in the marketing department would not have access to sensitive financial information.

Finally, it is vital that identity and access controls are dynamic and adaptive. In today's ever-evolving digital environment, threats change rapidly. Controls must therefore be regularly reviewed and adjusted to ensure that they remain effective in the face of new challenges and vulnerabilities.

Continuing with the fortified city analogy, think of identity and access controls as the guardians and sentinels that protect the castle – the heart of the city. Each entrance to the castle has a reinforced gate, and each gate is guarded by trained guards. These guards do not allow anyone to enter; They use specific lists and criteria to determine who may or may not enter.

Multi-factor authentication is like a system of triple checks that guards use. First, they may ask for a sign or password – something the visitor knows. Next, they may require the presentation of a badge or symbol – something that the visitor owns. And finally, they can recognize the visitor by their face or by some distinguishing mark – something that the visitor is. Only when all these checks are satisfied is access granted.

Also, not everyone who enters the castle has access to all its rooms and treasures. Depending on their role or purpose, they may be restricted to certain areas. A messenger, for example, would not have access to the treasure room. Similarly, role-based access controls ensure that organization members access only what is relevant to their responsibilities.

And just as guards are trained to be always vigilant, adapting to new tactics and threats from attackers, identity and access controls must also be dynamic. They must be updated and adapted as the threat landscape evolves, ensuring that the castle – the organization's protective surface – remains secure and tamper-proof.

5.6. Monitoring and Maintenance of the Solution

The journey to Zero Trust Privacy is continuous and dynamic. Once the solution is implemented, the real task begins: monitoring, assessing, and adapting to changes in the threat environment and organizational needs. Data security and privacy are not static; They require constant vigilance and frequent adjustments to stay ahead of emerging threats.

Proactive monitoring is key to quickly identifying and responding to any suspicious activity. This involves not only observing access attempts, but also deep analysis of network traffic, data transactions, and user behaviors.

Anomalies, even if subtle, can be indicative of intrusion attempts or system failures.

Artificial intelligence and machine learning play a crucial role in this scenario. These technologies can process vast amounts of data at staggering speeds, identifying patterns and trends that would be nearly impossible for humans to detect. By doing so, they can alert security teams to potential threats before they become real problems.

In addition to monitoring, regular maintenance of the Zero Trust Privacy solution is essential. This includes software updates, security patches, and access policy reviews. As the organization grows, changes, and adapts, the Zero Trust solution must evolve in parallel.

Finally, it is critical for organizations to maintain a mindset of continuous improvement. Regular training, attack simulation exercises, and policy reviews ensure that everyone involved is up to date on best practices and prepared to respond to incidents effectively. In a world where threats are constant and evolving, complacency is the enemy, and vigilance is the key to effective protection.

Continuing with the fortified city analogy, the monitoring and maintenance of the Zero Trust Privacy solution can be compared to the daily routine of a city that is always on alert. Imagine that the city walls have strategically placed watchtowers where sentinels watch the horizon 24/7. These sentries are always on the lookout for any suspicious movement, whether its distant dust indicating the approach of an army or a lone figure trying to sneak in.

Artificial intelligence and machine learning are like advanced sentinels equipped with long-range telescopes and listening devices. They can detect threats from afar, long before they get close to the city walls. And when they detect something, they sound the alarm, allowing the city to prepare and defend itself.

But walls and towers are not infallible. They wear and tear over time and need regular maintenance. Teams of builders and engineers inspect the defenses, repairing cracks, reinforcing weak points, and upgrading structures with new materials and technologies. Similarly, the Zero Trust Privacy solution needs to be constantly updated and adapted to face new threats.

And just as a city conducts battle drills and drills to keep its defenders fit and prepared, organizations should also conduct drills and drills to ensure their staff is ready to take on any challenge. In an ever-changing threat landscape, the city—or organization—that remains vigilant, adaptable, and always ready to learn and improve is the one that will remain safe and secure.

5.7. Zero Trust Privacy Maturity

Here we will explore the CISA Zero Trust Maturity Model, being a valuable tool that provides organizations with a clear roadmap to evaluate and enhance their approach to Zero Trust Privacy. Not only does this model highlight where an organization currently stands in its Zero Trust journey, but it also provides insights into next steps and areas that may need additional attention.

Each maturity level in the model represents a progressive stage in the implementation of Zero Trust Privacy. Starting with the basics and progressing to more sophisticated, proactive stages, organizations can use this model to identify gaps, prioritize initiatives, and align their efforts with industry best practices.

However, as with any significant transformation, the transition to Zero Trust Privacy comes with its set of challenges. Some of these obstacles are tangible, such as the need to invest in new technologies or adapt legacy infrastructure. Others are more intangible but equally critical, such as cultural resistance to change or a lack of clear understanding of Zero Trust principles among employees.

Resistance to change, in particular, can be one of the biggest obstacles. Many organizations have established cultures that value trust and openness. Introducing a "never trust, always check" mentality can be viewed with skepticism or concern. This is where education and awareness play a crucial role. Through training, workshops, and effective communication, organizations can help build an understanding and appreciation of the value and necessity of Zero Trust Privacy.

Ultimately, while the challenges are real, the benefits of a well-implemented Zero Trust Privacy approach are immense. By proactively recognizing and addressing challenges, organizations can ensure they are well-positioned to protect their most valuable data and assets in today's ever-evolving digital landscape.

Continuing with the fortified city analogy, the CISA Zero Trust Maturity Model can be likened to a detailed map that guides a city on its journey to becoming an impenetrable fortress. This map not only shows the current state of the city's defenses, but also highlights areas that can be strengthened and paths to achieving higher levels of security.

Each maturity level on the map represents a milestone in the evolution of the city's defenses. From building basic walls to implementing advanced watchtowers and deep moats, the city can follow this map to identify vulnerable areas and prioritize improvements.

However, fortifying a city is not an easy task. There may be difficult terrain, such as mountains or rivers, which make certain buildings challenging. Similarly, organizations may face tangible obstacles, such as legacy systems or a lack of resources. Furthermore, just as the citizens of a city can resist drastic changes in their familiar environment, the employees of an organization can be resistant to new approaches and mindsets.

The resistance to change, in this scenario, is similar to a city that has always had its gates open to all, valuing hospitality and trust. Closing these gates and introducing strict checks may be viewed with suspicion or fear by citizens. Therefore, it is essential for city leaders, or organizational leaders, to conduct awareness campaigns, showing the benefits of new defenses and the importance of adapting to new realities.

At the end of the day, while the challenges of turning an open city into a secure fortress are great, the benefits of protecting its citizens and their treasures are invaluable. With determination, planning, and the guidance of the map (or maturity model), the city can become a fortress of security in a world fraught with uncertainty.

5.8. Measuring the Success of Zero Trust Privacy

To assess the impact and effectiveness of Zero Trust Privacy, organizations need to establish clear metrics. These can include reducing risk, improving operational efficiency, and providing positive customer feedback.

Avoiding simple vanity metrics is critical in the Zero Trust Privacy journey. Business boards crave clear communications and impactful metrics that not only illustrate the strengths and weaknesses of their organization's security, but also demonstrate the effectiveness of the Zero Trust approach in protecting data privacy.

As modern organizations expand their networks, including integrations with cloud-based applications, the need for robust metrics that map security and operational performance becomes even more critical. These metrics should yield actionable insights, drive strategic decisions, and demonstrate the real value of Zero Trust Privacy.

When evaluating the success of Zero Trust Privacy, consider:

Business Impact: How do privacy metrics align with overall business objectives? Are they helping to mitigate risk and protect critical assets?

Trends Over Time: Monitoring the evolution of metrics can indicate the effectiveness of Zero Trust initiatives over time.

Benchmark Comparison: How do your organization's metrics compare to those of similar organizations that have also adopted Zero Trust Privacy?

Incident Response Time: How long does it take, on average, for the organization to identify and respond to a potential breach or suspicious activity? A faster response time can indicate an effective Zero Trust implementation and a well-trained security team.

User Satisfaction: How do users perceive the policies imposed by the company? Implementing Zero Trust Privacy must balance security with usability. Regular surveys or user feedback can provide valuable insights into areas of improvement.

False Positive Rate: How many alerts generated by the Zero Trust system turn out to be false positives? A high rate may indicate the need to refine the policies or technology in use.

Adapting to Evolving Threats: How is the organization adapting to new threats and trends? Zero Trust Privacy is not a one-size-fits-all solution; It must evolve as new threats emerge.

Training and Awareness: How many employees have been trained in Zero Trust policies and procedures in the last year? A well-informed workforce is the first line of defense against breaches.

These metrics, along with the traditional ones, provide a more holistic view of the effectiveness of implementing Zero Trust Privacy. By regularly monitoring and evaluating these metrics, organizations can identify areas for improvement, ensure compliance, and optimize data protection.

The Zero Trust Privacy approach is not just about adopting a new technology or tool, but rather about adopting an organizational mindset and culture that prioritizes data privacy and security across all operations. This mindset requires constant reassessment and the ability to adapt quickly to changes in the threat landscape and regulations.

Additionally, transparent communication of these metrics and findings to stakeholders is crucial. Stakeholders, whether they are employees, partners, or customers, need to understand the value of Zero Trust Privacy and how it benefits the organization and protects their data.

The success of implementing Zero Trust Privacy can also be measured by the organization's ability to maintain the trust of its stakeholders and proactively adapt to an ever-changing digital environment.

By embracing the ongoing Zero Trust journey and committing to constant assessment and improvement, organizations are well-positioned to meet the challenges of the future and protect the valuable data entrusted to them.

Continuing with the fortified city analogy, measuring the success of Zero Trust Privacy can be likened to a ruler evaluating the effectiveness of his city's defenses. It is not enough just to build high walls and deep moats; It is essential to constantly monitor the integrity of these defenses and the readiness of troops.

Imagine a king who, after fortifying his city, wants to know how well his defenses are working. It is not only based on the height of the walls or the depth of the moats. He notes how many invaders have been repelled, how quickly the guards respond to a threat, and how safe citizens feel inside the walls.

Business Impact: It is like assessing whether the city's commerce and economy are flourishing due to the sense of security provided by the defenses.

Trends Over Time: The king observes whether attacks on the city are decreasing over time and whether defenses are proving to be more robust.

Benchmark Comparison: The monarch may send spies or ambassadors to other cities to compare your defenses and tactics with theirs.

Incident Response Time: This is the time it takes for guards to respond to a threat on the walls or for archers to fire on an enemy.

User Satisfaction: The king consults his citizens. If they feel safe and secure, the defenses are working. If they feel restricted or inconvenient, adjustments may be necessary.

False Positive Rate: Sometimes, a guard may sound the alarm upon seeing a shadow, only to discover that it was a harmless animal. These are the false positives.

Adapting to Evolving Threats: Just as a king can upgrade his city's weapons and tactics in response to new siege methods, organizations must adapt to new digital threats.

Training and Awareness: The king ensures that all guards and citizens are well-trained and aware of defense protocols.

Just as a fortified city needs constant assessment and adjustment to ensure its security, organizations need to measure and adapt their Zero Trust Privacy approaches to ensure data protection. And just as citizen trust is vital to a city's success, stakeholder trust is crucial to an organization's success in the digital world.

6. Case Studies: Successes and Challenges

As you embark on the Zero Trust Privacy journey, each organization takes a distinct path, shaped by its culture, infrastructure, and goals. While some navigate turbulent seas of challenge, others discover more serene routes that lead to unexpected triumphs. Studying these individual trajectories offers a rich lesson learned, illuminating both winning strategies and potential obstacles. As we delve deeper into these case studies, we not only unlock the secrets of successful implementations, but also identify the red flags that can help other organizations navigate their own Zero Trust Privacy journey with more confidence.

In this context, we will present three distinct case studies, each reflecting a unique situation faced by organizations at distinct stages of their Zero Trust Privacy journey. We will examine instances ranging from a large financial company struggling to adapt its legacy infrastructure to a healthcare organization battling internal resistance, to a tech startup seeking harmony in a multi-cloud environment. These stories, while different in their detail, share common themes of challenge, innovation, and resilience. They serve as testaments to the adaptive spirit of organizations and the importance of a strategic approach when adopting Zero Trust Privacy. Let us explore each of these narratives and discover the rich lessons they have to offer.

Case 1: Adapting Legacy Infrastructure

A renowned financial institution in Europe, with more than 10,000 employees and systems dating back to the 1990s, faced the monumental challenge of integrating Zero Trust Privacy into its legacy infrastructure. With a traditional corporate culture and an established network across multiple branches, the main concern was the incompatibility of their old systems with the new security solutions. However, by taking a phased approach, they were able to create an additional layer of security. Collaboration between IT, security, and operations departments was crucial.

Case 2: Organizational Resistance to Zero Trust

A large hospital network in North America, with a culture of "openness" and "trust," has encountered significant resistance when introducing Zero Trust Privacy. With more than twenty hospitals under its management and a long history of fostering interdepartmental collaboration, the move to Zero Trust was viewed with skepticism. Leadership organized training sessions, demonstrating simulated cyberattacks and the associated risks. Over time, the organization has not only strengthened its security but also bolstered trust among employees and leadership.

Case 3: Implementation in a Multi-Cloud Environment

An innovative startup in the e-commerce sector in Southeast Asia, with a team of around two hundred people, faced the challenge of maintaining consistency in the implementation of Zero Trust Privacy across different platforms. Operating in a multi-cloud environment and with a culture of rapid innovation, each cloud provider had its own tools and interfaces. The solution came in the form of a unified security management platform, which allowed for policy setting in a central location.

As we reflect on these case studies, it becomes evident that the journey to Zero Trust Privacy is as diverse as the organizations undertaking it. Each story highlights the need for tailored approaches, tailored to each entity's specific circumstances and cultures. However, a unifying theme emerges: resilience and adaptability are key to overcoming the challenges inherent in implementing Zero Trust.

These cases also reinforce the idea that while technology and tools are vital components, the human element plays an equally crucial role. Collaboration, education, and communication is the backbone of any successful implementation.

I hope these stories serve as inspiration and guidance. May they illuminate possible paths, help anticipate obstacles and, above all, reinforce the idea that, with determination and strategy, Zero Trust Privacy is an achievable and valuable goal. In a world where data security is paramount, learning from the experiences of others is a vital step in building a safer and more reliable future for all.

It is highly recommended to delve deeper into benchmarks with industry peers, seeking insights and best practices. Engaging with recognized leaders in the subject can provide valuable perspective, allowing organizations to identify specific nuances and adapt accordingly to emerging trends. This collaborative approach not only enriches the implementation strategy, but also strengthens the network of professionals committed to data security and privacy.

7. Lessons Learned and Continuous Improvement

In any journey, especially those involving the implementation of new strategies or technologies, lessons learned play a key role in shaping future actions and decisions. Continuous improvement, in turn, is the process of using these lessons to make proactive adjustments and refinements, ensuring that processes become more efficient and effective over time.

7.1 Lessons Learned:

Lessons learned are like beacons on a dark night, illuminating the paths we walk and helping us avoid the same obstacles in the future. They are the essence of the experience, capturing the moments of challenge and triumph, allowing organizations to grow and evolve. Without acknowledging and reflecting on these lessons, we risk repeating the same mistakes, missing valuable opportunities for growth.

But how can we effectively capture these lessons and ensure that they are utilized for the benefit of the organization? A best practice is to create a centralized repository, a "logbook," where lessons learned are recorded, categorized, and easily accessible. This record should not just be a list of events, but rather a reflective analysis, highlighting what went right, what went wrong, and, most importantly, why.

Additionally, it is crucial to create an environment where teams feel comfortable sharing their experiences, both positive and negative. This can be achieved through regular review meetings, where team members discuss completed projects, challenges faced, and solutions found. These sessions not only foster a culture of continuous learning but also strengthen team cohesion as members come together to share knowledge and support each other.

Within these reflections and discussions, recurring themes emerge that stand out as pillars in the implementation of Zero Trust Privacy. They are:

Expectations vs. Reality: Often, what is expected of a new strategy or tool can differ from reality. Acknowledging this discrepancy and adjusting expectations can prevent frustration and ensure that goals are achieved in a more realistic manner.

Importance of Communication: Clear and transparent communication is vital. Whether it is between teams, departments, or with external stakeholders, ensuring everyone is on the same page prevents misunderstandings and makes implementation easier.

Flexibility is Essential: In an ever-changing world, the ability to quickly adapt to new challenges or changes in the environment is crucial. Organizations that are rigid in their approach may encounter difficulties when faced with unexpected obstacles.

7.2 Continuous Improvement:

At the heart of any successful Zero Trust Privacy initiative is the idea of continuous improvement. In an ever-evolving digital environment, complacency can be the biggest enemy. Thus, it is vital for organizations to not only implement strategies but also review and improve them regularly. Let us explore some essential topics that can serve as catalysts for enhancing continuous improvement.

Regular Evaluation: Continuous improvement begins with evaluation. This involves reviewing processes, strategies, and results regularly to identify areas of potential improvement.

Implementing Feedback: Feedback, whether it is from customers, employees, or data analytics, is a valuable source of information. Using this feedback to make proactive adjustments can lead to better results in the long term.

Training and Development: As new lessons are learned, it is essential that teams and individuals receive ongoing training and development. This ensures that everyone is equipped with the necessary skills and knowledge to take on future challenges.

Learning Culture: Fostering a culture where learning and innovation are valued can encourage individuals to constantly seek ways to improve and innovate.

Lessons learned offer valuable insights that can guide and shape future actions. When combined with a continuous improvement mindset, these lessons become the foundation for ensuring that organizations constantly move forward, adapt, and improve, no matter what challenges arise.

Continuous improvement is more than just a practice; it is a philosophy. Organizations that embrace it are not only better prepared to face the challenges of the present, but also position themselves solidly to face the challenges of the future with confidence and skill. By adopting this approach, organizations can ensure that their Zero Trust Privacy strategy remains robust, relevant, and resilient, regardless of the changes that the future may bring.

8. The Future and Global Regulations of Zero Trust Privacy

As technology advances, so does the way we approach privacy and security. Zero Trust Privacy, while a relatively new approach, is already seeing innovations and adaptations that promise to shape its future.

Advancements in Artificial Intelligence (AI) and Machine Learning (ML): AI and ML are becoming crucial tools in proactive threat detection and incident response. In the context of Zero Trust, these technologies can be used to monitor behavior patterns, identify suspicious activity, and respond in real-time to potential breaches.

Privacy as a Service: As organizations recognize the importance of Zero Trust Privacy, new services are emerging that offer privacy-as-a-service solutions. These solutions allow companies to implement Zero Trust practices without the need to develop in-house infrastructures.

At the same time, the global regulatory landscape is constantly evolving. Countries around the world are updating or introducing new privacy laws, many of which incorporate Zero Trust principles. For example, the European Union's General Data Protection Regulation (GDPR) and Brazil's General Data Protection Law (LGPD) are reflections of this global trend of prioritizing data privacy. Regardless of jurisdiction, the global trend is clear: data privacy is a priority. Zero Trust Privacy, with its rigorous and principled approach, can help organizations navigate this complex and ever-changing regulatory landscape.

In addition, many organizations operate in hybrid environments, combining on-premises infrastructures with cloud solutions. Implementing Zero Trust in these complex environments presents unique challenges, from identity management to network segmentation.

As we look to the future of Zero Trust Privacy, it is evident that the approach will continue to evolve and adapt. Organizations that want to stay at the forefront of privacy and security will need to be mindful of these trends and ready to adapt their strategies as needed.

9. Conclusion: The Road Ahead to Zero Trust Privacy

Zero Trust Privacy transcends mere technique to become a philosophy that resonates with the urgency to rethink our approach to privacy and security in the contemporary digital landscape. In an era where every click, every online interaction, can be a vector for threats, the maxim "never trust, always verify" is not just a recommendation, but a necessity.

Throughout this eBook, we navigate the details of Zero Trust Privacy, from its theoretical conception to its practical application, illustrated by case studies that demonstrate both the challenges and the triumphs. This journey reiterated an incontrovertible truth: in a world where data is compared to gold, its meticulous protection is necessary.

Cultural resistance, often rooted in traditional practices and mentalities, is undoubtedly an obstacle. However, as highlighted, the solution to this resistance lies in education and awareness-raising. Through workshops, training, and awareness campaigns, it is possible to create an organizational culture where Zero Trust is not seen as an imposition, but as a necessary evolution.

Technical complexity, especially in organizations that still operate with legacy systems, is another challenge. But, as discussed, the incremental approach, starting with the most critical areas and gradually expanding, can ease this transition. And, with the range of tools and technologies we have at our disposal today, adopting Zero Trust becomes a viable proposition.

Investing in Zero Trust Privacy may seem costly at first. However, when weighing the risks associated with not adopting this approach – from data breaches to regulatory repercussions – it is clear that the investment may be justified.

Usability is another key pillar. After all, security should not compromise the user experience. With innovations in authentication, such as context-based multi-factor authentication, you can reconcile robust security with a seamless user experience.

To conclude, Zero Trust Privacy is not a destination, but a journey of constant adaptation and learning. As the threat landscape transforms, strategies to combat them must also evolve. Organizations that embrace Zero Trust Privacy not only strengthen their advocacy but also position themselves as the vanguard in an ever-evolving digital world. The journey can be challenging, but with Zero Trust as a compass, the path becomes clearer and the journey undoubtedly rewarding.

Additional Resources and References

In this eBook, I took a deep dive into the concept of Zero Trust Privacy. To ensure the accuracy and relevance of the information, I turned to a number of reliable sources. Below are the citations and references that I found pertinent. If you are interested in further expanding your knowledge or seeking additional resources on this topic, the following links may be of terrific value:

- FORRESTER. The Definition of Modern Zero Trust. Available at: https://www.forrester.com/blogs/the-definition-of-modern-zero-trust/. Accessed on: June 8, 2023.

- THE WHITE HOUSE. Executive Order on Improving the Nation's Cybersecurity. Available at: https://www.whitehouse.gov/briefing-room/presidential-actions/2021/05/12/executive-order-on-improving-the-nations-cybersecurity/. Accessed on: June 14, 2023.

- GARTNER. Zero Trust Network Access (ZTNA). Available at: https://www.gartner.com/en/information-technology/glossary/zero-trust-network-access-ztna-. Accessed on: June 15, 2023.

- CISA - Zero Trust Maturity Model (PDF). Available at: https://www.cisa.gov/sites/default/files/2023-04/zero_trust_maturity_model_v2_508.pdf. Accessed on: July 5. 2023.

- ISACA NEWSLETTERS. The Challenges and Rewards of Zero Trust Privacy. Available at: https://www.isaca.org/resources/news-and-trends/newsletters/atisaca/2023/volume-28/the-challenges-and-rewards-of-zero-trust-privacy. Accessed on: June 30, 2023.

- NIST. NIST Special Publication 800-207. Available at: https://nvlpubs.nist.gov/nistpubs/SpecialPublications/NIST.SP.800-207.pdf. Accessed on: 12 de Jul. 2023.

- ISACA JOURNAL. Zero Trust in Data Privacy Operations. Available at: https://www.isaca.org/resources/isaca-journal/issues/2022/volume-3/zero-trust-in-data-privacy-operations. Accessed on: July 18. 2023.

- SANS INSTITUTE. What is Zero Trust Architecture?. Available at: https://www.sans.org/blog/what-is-zero-trust-architecture/. Accessed on: 25 de Jul. 2023.

- YOUTUBE. Zero Trust and the Power of Identity. Available at:

https://www.youtube.com/watch?v=tYyEpQEFHOg &t=1s. Accessed on: July 22. 2023.

- STORJ. Zero Trust is Critical to Security & Privacy in Decentralized Systems. Available at: https://www.storj.io/blog/zero-trust-is-critical-to-security-privacy-in-decentralized-systems. Accessed on: Aug. 3. 2023.

- ISACA. Mastering a Zero Trust Security Strategy. Available at: https://www.isaca.org/resources/mastering-a-zero-trust-security-strategy. Accessed on: 7 de ago. 2023.

- CISA. Zero Trust Maturity Model. Available at: https://www.cisa.gov/zero-trust-maturity-model. Accessed on: 10 de ago. 2023.

Questions for Reflection

1. How can the Zero Trust Privacy philosophy be implemented to my organization?
2. What are the main challenges my organization faces regarding data security and privacy?
3. What are my organization's current security practices and how do they align with Zero Trust Privacy principles?
4. How can we foster a culture of data security awareness and education within our team?
5. What are the regulatory and legal implications that my organization should consider when implementing Zero Trust Privacy?
6. What is the role of executive leadership in the successful adoption of Zero Trust Privacy?
7. What metrics and performance indicators are relevant to track the effectiveness of our Zero Trust Privacy strategy?
8. How can we ensure usability and user experience by implementing stringent security measures?
9. What is the strategic value of investing in Zero Trust Privacy, considering the potential risks of not doing so?
10. What are the next steps for my organization in the Zero Trust Privacy adoption journey?

Glossary

Data-Centric Approach: A strategy that emphasizes data in security and privacy decisions.

Multi-Cloud Environment: Use of multiple cloud solutions from different providers by an organization.

Hybrid environments: Combining on-premises infrastructures with cloud solutions.

Cyberattacks: Malicious acts against data, networks, or digital systems.

Continuous Authentication: Continuous verification of identity during sessions.

Multi-Factor Authentication (MFA): Security that requires multiple forms of verification.

Context-based multi-factor authentication: Verification of identity using multiple factors.

Security Breaches: Incidents where security systems are compromised, leading to an unauthorized exposure or loss of data.

Personal Data: Information that can be used to directly or indirectly identify a person, such as name, address, date of birth, or IP address.

Digital Age: Contemporary period characterized by the prevalence and dependence on digital technologies, the internet, and automation in various spheres of life and business.

Security Evolution: The continuous process of adapting and improving security measures to address new threats and challenges.

Fair Information Practice Principles (FIPPs): Principles of information protection and privacy.

Feedback: Comments or feedback for adjustments or improvements.

Firewalls: Devices for monitoring and filtering network traffic.

Privacy Management: Administration of personal data collected, stored, and protected.

Identity management: Process for managing identifications, authentications, and authorizations in systems.

GDPR (General Data Protection Regulation): European regulation for the protection of personal data.

Hardware: Physical components of a computer or system, such as the motherboard, processor, and RAM.

Identification of Privacy Risks: Identification of vulnerabilities in data privacy.

IT Infrastructure: Components for IT operations and services.

Artificial Intelligence (AI): Simulation of human functions, such as learning and decision-making.

IoT (Internet of Things): Connected devices for data collection and analysis.

LGPD (General Data Protection Law): Brazilian regulation for the protection of personal data.

Machine Learning (ML): Machines that learn and decide from data.

Security Patches: Updates to fix vulnerabilities in software.

Digital Footprint: Trace left by digital activities.

Centralized Repository: Primary location for data storage and access.

Cybersecurity: Protection against digital threats.

Information Security: Measures to protect information from unwanted access or damage.

Network segmentation: Creating subnets for better performance and security.

Stakeholders: Entities interested in the results of an organization.

Software: A set of instructions and data processed by hardware, allowing specific tasks to be performed on a computer or other electronic device.

Digital Transformation: Integration of digital technology into business processes.

U.S. Department of Health, Education, and Welfare: U.S. government department.

Data Breaches: Incidents of unauthorized access to information.

Zero Trust: Principle that does not automatically trust any entity, regardless of origin.

Zero Trust Privacy: Principle that is based on the idea of not automatically trusting any entity inside or outside an organization when it comes to data privacy. This model requires constant verification and revalidation of trust across all data access points.

Thank You Page

A Sincere Thank You

As I delve deeper into the world of digital security, I realize that true understanding comes not only from technical knowledge, but also from the valuable contributions and understandings of diverse people and sources.

I wish to express my deepest gratitude to everyone who has dedicated their time, effort, and knowledge to make this e-book a reality. To the experts who shared their experiences, to the reviewers who provided constructive feedback, and to the many researchers whose ongoing work in the field of digital security has served as the foundation for this content.

To you, reader, my gratitude for trusting me, for seeking understanding, and for your passion for protecting the digital world. This e-book is an outcome of my commitment to providing quality information and will hopefully be a useful tool in your journey.

In the ever-changing digital world, collaboration and knowledge sharing are more crucial than ever. Thank you for being a part of this community and for helping me move forward.

Last, but certainly not least, a special thanks to the research pages that were instrumental in carrying out this work. Without the availability of these sources, the deepening and breadth of this e-book would not be possible.

Moreover, I cannot express my gratitude to my wife, who played a key role in the construction and revision of this book. Their dedication and support have been invaluable.

Thank you all so much!

Connect & Share!

Hello, dear reader!

If you have made it this far, I sincerely hope you have enjoyed and benefited from the content in this eBook. Your opinion is paramount to me. If you have feedback, insights, or personal stories related to the topic, I would love to hear all about it.

Also, if you have found value in the information and insights presented, consider sharing the eBook in your network. This can help others benefit from this information, just like you.

To reach out to me directly, discuss ideas, share feedback, or simply connect professionally, go to my LinkedIn, and send me a message. I look forward to hearing from you!
https://www.linkedin.com/in/nandorfeher/

Thank you for reading and for being a part of this journey with me. Hope to talk to you soon!

Nandor Feher
CISO & DPO